Poetic Letters From God

Messages of Hope, Faith and Transformation

Shruti Alok

Made with ❤ on the BookLeaf Publishing Platform
www.bookleafpub.in
www.bookleafpub.com

Dedication

To those on a journey of healing, may these words bring you comfort, strength and the peace that comes from within. I dedicate this book to the divine presence of God, whose grace, guidance and love made this work possible. Without God, these words would not have come to life.

Preface

In the quiet moments of reflection, when the world around me seemed still, I began to hear a voice - a gentle whisper, a guiding force that spoke directly to my soul. These were not mere thoughts, but messages, pure and divine, reminding me of the love, hope and healing that resides within us all. It is with deep humility and immense gratitude that I share this collection of poetry, Poetic Letters From God.

This book is not only a journey of words but a spiritual experience meant to guide, comfort and heal. Each poem is a letter - a direct communication from the divine for those navigating the challenges of life. Through this verses I invite you to open your heart, to embrace the peace that flows through every word and connect with divine presence that never leaves us.

I write these poems with profound gratitude for God, whose presence is the source of every breath I take and whose grace made the very act of writing this book possible. Without his guidance, this journey would not have been possible.
These words are a gift, and it is my hope that they will serve as a balm for your spirit, as a reminder of the

divine love that is always with you, guiding you towards healing and peace.

May these letters offer you solace in times of sorrow, strength in moments of weakness, and unwavering knowledge that you are never alone. For in every verse, there is message of love, healing and divine presence waiting to touch your heart.

With love and gratitude,
Shruti Alok

Acknowledgements

I would like to express my deepest gratitude to all who have supported and inspired me on spiritual journey. May these letters bring peace and encouragement to all those who read them.

1. You are sun , Keep Shining

Badalo Ke Andhkar ke
Bhaay ke karan

Ye mat bhulo
ke tum

" Surya Ho "

English Trans :

Darling ,

You fear the clouds ?
You forgot

You are
" The Sun "

2. No, Your experience might be different

No

My dear

There experience cannot be yours

Even if the road is same.

Experience differs

Do not mistake their experience of things as your

The path that is difficult may be easy for some

And the path that is easy
May be hard for some

3. Playful mind

Agar mushkil raste ko asaan
Nahi maana

Toh asaan rasta bhi
Mushkil lagega

Chanchal Maan

English translation :

If you don't take
Difficult road (situation) easily

Then even the easiest road (situation)
You will feel difficult

That playful mind .

4. Patience

Dhyan apne apme
Dhairya ki pariksha

Dhairya apne apme
Shaurya ki pariksha

English translation :

For meditation itself
Examines patience

And patience itself
Examines

" Bravery " .

5. For new you. Forget the old " YOU "

Praise yourself
In order to raise yourself

Erase yourself
In order to

Praise yourself.

6. Roots

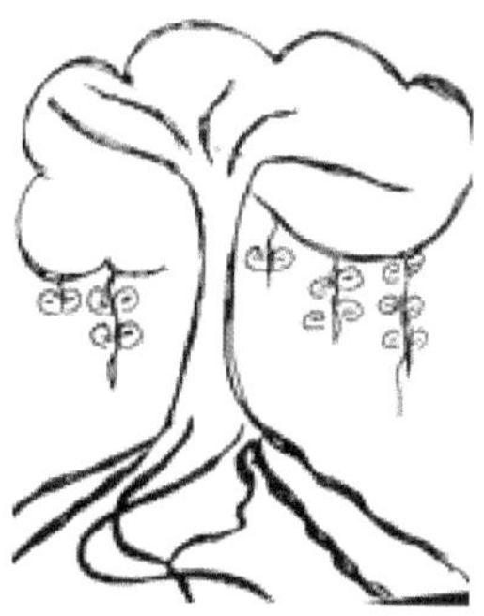

The more the understanding of roots
The more the standing of tree .

7. Ahhh! My dear they simply cannot see

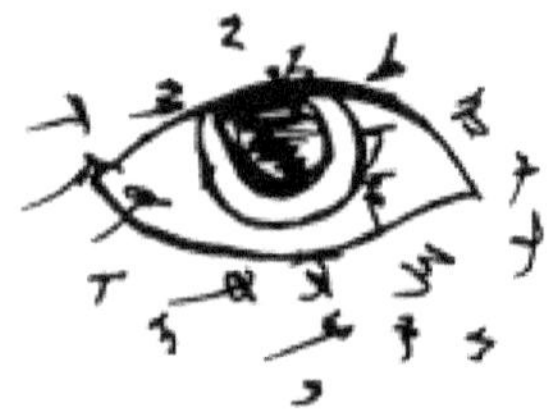

It's not that
You are wrong

It's simply that
They see no right
Through their real eyes
Because their eyes are
Covered with flies

So they are unable to
See their own vibe
Then how can they

Understand your

" LIGHT " ?

8. Tears can be colourful as well

In order to paint
Paintbrush has to be

Wet first

Want to make life colourful ?
Yet afraid of tears......

9. Lost & found

Remember,

Nothing is ever lost in life
Whatever is lost

Is a gain
In " Another Form " .

10. Their karma. You Angry ?

Don't burn yourself
In anger

Because of
Someone else wrong karma
Towards you

Remember
It's their karma

Your response is
Yours..

11. Wheel of karma

Karma ka chakra
Kuch is prakar chala

Waqt ne
Kisiko bure karma ka
Fal de dia

Use pata bhi na chala

English trans :

The wheel of karma
Turned in a way
One who did " Bad deed "
Got his fruit

He got no idea about.

12. Clay/ Sand/ Dust at the end

Mitti se banta insaan hai
Mitti se banta matka hai

Insaan,

Chahe jo bhi akaar le
Chahe jo bhi vichar le

Mitti me mil jata hai.

English translation :

Pot
Made from clay
So the human

Human,
That flesh - what so ever shape
Those thoughts - which so ever waves
Will all crash

In the end
And merge to same " CLAY ".

13. You are your armour

Har kahani
Teri pariksha hai

Tu swayam hi
Teri raksha hai .

English translation :

Each story you live in life
Is your test

You and only you
Can protect " YOU "

14. Warrior

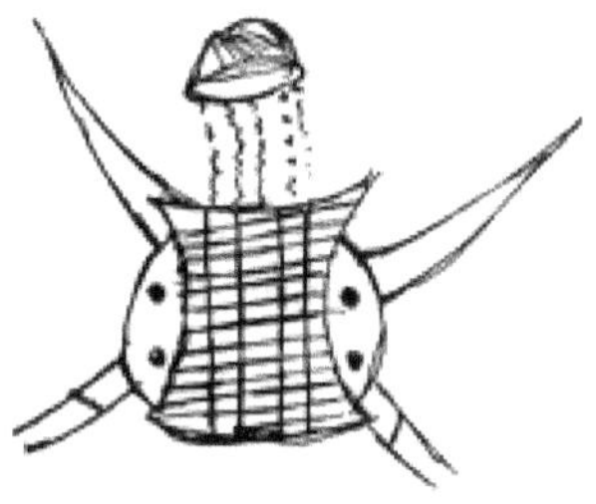

Warrior is the one
Who knows

When there is need of peace
And when there is need of war

Balance mind

15. God's answer

My Dear,

To few questions of yours
I answer
Through your inner voice

To some other questions
I answer
Through other person's mouth

If you understand that
You got your answer

If you don't understand that
Even the answer
Becomes

Your question...

NO QUESTION UNANSWERED BY GOD

16. Choice

Choice is yours
Boat is yours
Want to swim or drown

Result yours.... LIFE

17. Darling! You cannot hold everything

Want to catch sand ?
It will slip away from your hand

Want to catch water ?
Oh the drops will pass away

Want to catch fire ?
Beware !! You will burn

Want to catch air ?
Haha ! Try your luck

Ever thought
You made of these five elements
Cannot catch a single element

And you want to catch LIFE ?
FLOW > FORCE

My darling
FLOW IS GREATER THEN FORCE.

24

18. Real Love

Soul to soul love
What is it ?

Love where the unknown is
Already known
Love where known
Becomes unknown

Love where emotions are highest vibe
Not the reason behind pride

Love where action itself
Is the direction

Love where faith is bigger then fear
Love that is rare & when you find it
Whole universe

Declares.

19. Timing

Time take it's own beauty
You just need wait
Do your duty

Today it might not rain
Does that mean each day is drought ?

Oh baby
Don't cry that heart
Don't shout that is your insult

If today there is no water enough
For your boat to cross

Tommorow there will be land enough
To guide your each step

Across the sea.

20. Cage

No matter how many pilgrimage you go
Mind with bad thoughts
Action of bad deeds

Then you are still in
" CAGE " .

21. Traveller

I am a traveller (wanderer) friends
on this earth,
I am on a journey, journey of finding myself
I am aware of my beginning with dust
I am aware of my end in dust (ashes)

All I am unaware of is the journey
Wanderer I am

Just a space between
A line between birth and death I am.